Resolving
Grievances

By Daniel Barnett

The Employment Law Library

All books in the Employment Law Library are sent for free to members of the HR Inner Circle.

1. Employee Investigations

2. GDPR for HR Professionals

3. Preventing and Defending Employee Stress Claims

4. Employment Tribunal Time Limits

5. Deconstructing TUPE

6. Changing Terms & Conditions

7. Constructive Dismissal

8. Resolving Grievances

Published by Employment Law Services Limited, Unit 3, Chequers Farm, Chequers Lane, Watford, Hertfordshire WD25 0LG

EMPLOYMENT
LAW
MATTERS

GETTING REDUNDANCY RIGHT

MODULE 1:	Introduction
MODULE 2:	Definition of Redundancy and Challenging
MODULE 3:	Avoiding Redundancies
MODULE 4:	Choosing your selection pool
MODULE 5:	Choosing your selection criteria
MODULE 6:	Scoring and individual consultation
MODULE 7:	Collective consultation
MODULE 8:	Alternative employment
MODULE 9:	Dismissal
MODULE 10:	Miscellaneous issues

THESE BONUS RESOURCES ARE AVAILABLE IN THE VAULT TO ALL PURCHASERS OF GETTING REDUNDANCY RIGHT:

One complimentary place at Daniel Barnett's next 'HR Secrets' seminar tour (the previous tour took place in 15 cities around the UK, with topics including holiday pay, spotting malingering, and top mistakes made by HR Professionals)
FIRST 100 PURCHASERS ONLY | Value: £120

Daniel Barnett's template redundancy selection matrix, which you can use to score employees during a selection process
Value: £75

Daniel Barnett's redundancy policy, which he uses with his regular corporate clients
Value: £100

Private online forum, where you can discuss issues arising from redundancies and ask questions
Value: £125

3 x live Zoom Q&A sessions with expert guest speakers on redundancy
Value: £100

Access to videos of 31 webinars chaired by Daniel Barnett in early 2020, with 31 employment barristers on 31 aspects of employment law
Value: £60

WWW.GETTINGREDUNDANCYRIGHT.COM

DANIEL BARNETT
BARRISTER

THE UK'S LEADING YOUTUBE CHANNEL FOR LAW EXPLAINER VIDEOS

BIT.LY/**YOUTUBELEGAL**

About the Author

Daniel Barnett is a leading employment law barrister practising from Outer Temple Chambers. With 25 years' experience defending public and private sector employers against employment claims, he has represented a Royal Family, several international airlines, FTSE-100 companies and various NHS Trusts and local authorities. Employee clients include David & Victoria Beckham's nanny and Paul Mason (subject of the ITV documentary 'Britain's Fattest Man').

Daniel is a past chair of the Employment Lawyers' Association's publishing committee and electronic services working party. He is the author or co-author of eight books, including the Law Society Handbook on Employment Law (currently in its 8th edition). He is the creator of the Employment Law (UK) mailing list, an email alerter bulletin service sending details of breaking news in employment law three times a week to 30,000 recipients.

Legal directories describe him as 'extremely knowledgeable and [he] can absorb pages of instructions at lightning speed', 'involved in a number of highly contentious matters', 'singled out for his work for large blue-chip companies', 'combination of in-depth legal knowledge, pragmatism, quick response times and approachability', 'inexhaustible', 'tenacious', 'knowledgeable', and 'an excellent advocate'.

He is one of the leading speakers and trainers on the employment law and HR circuit. He has presented seminars for the House of Commons, the BBC, Oxford University, HSBC, Barclays Bank, Ocado, and dozens of other organisations in-house. In 2013, 2014, 2016, and 2019 he designed — and was the sole speaker at — the Employment Law MasterClass national tour.

As well as full-time practice as a barrister and speaker, Daniel is the founder of the HR Inner Circle – a membership club for smart, ambitious HR Professionals. In 2007, he co-founded CPD Webinars Ltd, then the UK's leading webinar training company for lawyers, and sold it to Thomson Reuters in 2011.

Daniel is widely sought after as a commentator in both broadcast and print media on all legal issues. Since 2010 he has presented the Legal Hour on LBC Radio. In 2019, he launched Employment Law Matters, a weekly podcast with short explanations of employment law topics. Subscribe at www.danielbarnett.co.uk/podcast

www.danielbarnett.co.uk
Outer Temple Chambers
Strand, London

Acknowledgments

This is the eighth in my series of small employment law books. They are designed to give HR professionals and those without a formal law degree a solid grounding in a subject that they won't learn about through normal avenues. The content is at a similar level to undergraduate LLB degree courses, so anyone who is familiar with this book will know as much as any junior lawyer.

I'd like to thank Kathy Daniels for her help with the content, Eugenie Verney for proofreading, Jennie Hargrove for editing, Tincuta Moscaliuc for the layout and design and Maria Rodriguez for converting the book to the formats needed for Amazon.

I would also like to thank Penelope Douglass, Rebecca Gott, Janell White, Lorna Mapson, Susi O'Brien, Jean Hall, Patrick McNamee, Alison Lambert and, in particular, Quentin Colborn, all of whom brought their many years' experience as HR professionals to bear when sharing their comments on an early draft of this book so as to enhance the content. All are members of www.hrinnercircle. co.uk and I learn as much from them as I hope they learn from me.

Finally, I wish to thank Paul Helsby, also a member of www.hrinnercircle.co.uk. I have adopted several of the concepts from his book, 'You don't have to shout...or do you? How to effectively manage workplace grievances', and recommend you buy a copy from bit.ly/youdonthavetoshout

Daniel Barnett
December 2020

Table of Contents

CHAPTER 1
Defining a grievance

What is a grievance?

It's more than a grumble, a moan or general discontent. However we define the word 'grievance' (and there is no formal legal definition), there is an important distinction between moaning and a formal grievance. If an employee has raised a grievance, then the employee is sufficiently dissatisfied to want to give the situation some formality. 'Raising a grievance' is much more significant than moaning about work on a Monday morning.

As we will see when we explore the Acas Code of Practice on Disciplinary and Grievance Procedures, there is an expectation that an employee will put a grievance into writing. However, this might not always be as clear as putting the matter in a letter which specifically labels the situation as a grievance.

It is important to remember that your duty to resolve/deal with a grievance does not mean you have to resolve/deal with it to the employee's satisfaction. You merely need to resolve/deal with it fairly. Sometimes, the employee may remain dissatisfied. But as long as you've dealt with the grievance fairly and reasonably, you'll have done what the law (and good employment practice) requires of you.

In reality, there will always be something that employees can complain about at work. However, most of the time most people accept that the world isn't perfect, and let minor issues go, because they're just not worth complaining about. Not everyone is the same. Some complain more than others. But usually, if somebody complains, it is because they think that they have a genuine grievance or complaint. Most grievances have an element of truth; it is very rare that they are entirely without foundation.

Between 2004 and 2009, there was a short-lived law that required employees to raise a grievance before they could sue their employers for many employment claims. That led to courts considering what was meant by a 'grievance'. The courts tended to be very relaxed about the definition, almost to the point of labelling any complaint in writing (including resignation letters) a grievance so as not to deny employees the opportunity to bring tribunal claims. Although the cases have never been formally overruled, nobody relies on them nowadays.

Does a grievance have to be dealt with?

From a 'good practice' point of view, a grievance should always be dealt with because if it is ignored, there is a real likelihood that the situation will escalate into something more serious, such as a legal claim or other employees joining in the complaint.

There is also a legal risk involved in ignoring a grievance. The most likely risk is that an employee whose grievance is ignored goes on to resign and claim constructive dismissal. However, an employee might also claim that the employer's decision to ignore their grievance was discriminatory, or perhaps claim on grounds of whistleblowing or some other protected characteristic.

The following cases illustrate the importance of addressing/considering grievances promptly and correctly:

> **WA Goold (Pearmak) Ltd v McConnell and another [1995] IRLR 516**
>
> Two sales representatives were paid a basic salary and commission. The business started

to decline due to the Managing Director being ill, which meant that the sales representatives earned less money. A new Managing Director was appointed, and the sales representatives met with him to discuss their declining salaries. The Managing Director said nothing could be done.

The sales representatives' solicitor wrote to the organisation asking for assurances about salary levels, which were not given. An offer was then made which meant that the sales representatives' salaries would be £5,000 lower. The sales representatives asked to discuss the situation with the Company Chairman but their line manager obstructed their attempts to meet with him. Their grievance went unresolved – in the sense the company simply didn't deal with it – for about three months. The sales representatives resigned and successfully claimed constructive dismissal.

The Employment Appeal Tribunal stated that all employers are required to reasonably and promptly give a reasonable opportunity to their employees to obtain redress of any grievance which they might have. Making the sales representatives wait for three months and leaving the grievance unresolved was not sufficiently prompt, and it therefore amounted to a constructive dismissal.

Bracebridge Engineering Ltd v Darby [1990] IRLR 3

An employee was sexually assaulted at work by two male supervisors. She reported the assault to the General Manager who took no action against the men. She resigned and successfully claimed sex discrimination and constructive dismissal. Her grievance had not been addressed.

What if someone other than the employee raises the grievance?

In most cases, an aggrieved employee will raise the grievance, but there could be situations in which someone raises the grievance on the aggrieved employee's behalf. This could be because the employee is so upset about the situation that they are unable to talk about what has happened. It could be because the employee is nervous about the reaction of the employer, feels intimidated, and fears that raising a grievance could make matters worse.

If someone raises a grievance on behalf of an employee, it should still be addressed. It does not matter who raises the grievance; it can be from a colleague (although you should check that the employee knows about it and genuinely does want the matter to be investigated) or even the employee's lawyer.

Sometimes, the grievance will be raised by the employee's union representative. You should deal with it as if it came from the employee themselves, but communicate (as a first port of call) with the union representative. Most good union officials won't support something that isn't a genuine grievance, for three reasons:

- the union representative would be raising expectations that they would be unable to fulfil (i.e. achieve a satisfactory resolution to) if it wasn't a genuine, live grievance.

- it would damage the union representative's credibility with management, as they might start to question the union representative's judgment.

- filing frivolous or inappropriate issues with management can, over time, destroy the union representative's relationship with the company, which would make resolving larger issues more difficult.

> ### Arnold Clark Automobiles Ltd v Stewart (2005) UKEATS/0052/05
>
> Stewart was the General Manager when the business was sold, and the new owners intended to appoint a different General Manager. There was no discussion with Stewart, so he resigned and claimed constructive dismissal. His solicitor wrote a letter on his behalf, setting out the concerns. This was ruled to be a grievance letter, even though it did not come from the employee himself.

What should your grievance policy say?

Your grievance policy should set out what the employee has to do to raise a grievance, and it should say who the employee should send their grievance letter to. Typically, this will be the employee's line manager. Employees should be encouraged to use email where appropriate.

I recommended that you also give the employee the option of raising their grievance with another manager or the HR department. The main reason for this is that the line manager might be the subject of the complaint! From April 2020, new employee written statements of particulars of employment must set out the person with whom grievances should usually be raised. Make sure that statements of particulars of employment and your grievance policy say the same thing.

Ideally, the grievance should set out in clear language exactly what the employee's complaint is, any evidence they rely on or any witnesses to the incident(s), and state what action they want you to take as a result (for example: 'I would like you to discipline my line manager', or 'I would like you to change my working pattern so I don't need to work on Tuesdays'). You can see below how this is dealt with in the model grievance policy in Appendix 1.

> 3.1 You will need to set out the details of your complaint in writing. Include dates, names of individuals involved, and any other relevant facts, and tell us clearly that you want to lodge a formal grievance. It will be helpful if you set out any steps you have taken to resolve the issue informally.
>
> 3.2 You must also explain clearly what you want to see the Company do. You could, for example, say: 'I want you to issue a warning to (the name of the individual you are complaining about)', or: 'I want you to change your policy on overtime working.'

3.3 Send or hand your written grievance to [your line manager] [or] [the HR department]. If your line manager is part of your grievance, you should send your grievance to [their line manager, or to] [NAME].

CHAPTER 2

The Acas Code of Practice on Disciplinary and Grievance Procedures

The Acas Code of Practice on Disciplinary and Grievance Procedures ('the Code of Practice') is a statutory code expressly approved by Parliament which sets out how a grievance should be managed. Not following the Code of Practice does not mean that the employer has definitely acted unlawfully. However, if the situation should subsequently result in a claim being made to an employment tribunal, any lack of adherence to the Code of Practice will be taken into account. It's a little like the Highway Code a breach of the Highway Code does not automatically mean someone is driving negligently, but it's a strong indicator. Likewise, a breach of the Code of Practice does not automatically mean someone has been constructively dismissed, or unfairly dismissed, but it's a strong indicator.

Departing from the procedures set out in the Code of Practice is not simply something that could lead to potential liability for an employer; it can also affect the amount of compensation the aggrieved employee receives. In the event of any unreasonable failure by an employer to follow the Code of Practice, any compensation awarded in relation to the situation can be increased by up to 25%. If the employee has unreasonably failed to follow the guidance set out in the Code of Practice, an employment tribunal can reduce the award by up to 25%.

The Code of Practice uses the phrase 'grievance hearing' and 'grievance meeting' interchangeably. It's a bit confusing, as one sounds more formal than the other, but they mean the same thing. Following that convention (or lack of convention), I also use the words 'hearing' and 'meeting' interchangeably in this book.

Introduction to the Code of Practice

The Code of Practice starts with some simple guidance. In summary, it states:

- Employers should always try to resolve grievance situations within the workplace.

- If this is not possible, employers should seek help from an independent third party (e.g. a mediator). This might be someone outside the organisation, but it could be someone who works in the organisation who is not involved in any way with the situation.

- Many situations can be resolved informally, with a quiet word. Always try that before the situation becomes formal.

- Act reasonably and fairly.

- Keep a written record of any grievance situation.

- It might be useful to have a separate procedure for specific situations such as bullying, harassment or whistleblowing.

I will explore these in more detail throughout this book.

General principles of the Code of Practice

The Code of Practice goes on to set out some general principles of managing a grievance. (The Code of Practice also addresses disciplinary issues and the general principles relating to them, but I do not focus on them in this book.)

1. Grievances are concerns, problems or complaints that employees raise with their employers.

2. Fairness and transparency come from developing rules and procedures. Set out grievance procedures in writing and involve employees and/or their representatives in the process of writing them. Employees should know what the procedures are and where they can be found.

3. The action to be taken will depend on the facts of the case. When deciding if an employer has acted reasonably, an employment tribunal will take into account the size and resources of the employer.

4. A grievance situation should be addressed fairly. Specifically, the Code of Practice says:

   • employers and employees should raise and deal with issues promptly and should not unreasonably delay meetings, decisions or confirmation of those decisions.

   • employers and employees should act consistently.

   • employers should carry out any investigations necessary to establish the facts of the case.

- employers should allow employees to be accompanied at any formal grievance meeting.

- employers should allow employees to appeal against any formal decision made.

Any company grievance procedure should be followed. Most will be based on the Code of Practice, and grievance procedures for larger companies (or those that have been agreed with unions) will normally expand on the Code of Practice and provide extra levels of detail and investigation. There is a model grievance policy in Appendix 1, which you are welcome to use or adapt.

CHAPTER 3

Initial response when receiving a grievance

Paragraph 32 of the Code of Practice states:

"If it is not possible to resolve a grievance informally, employees should raise the matter formally and without unreasonable delay with a manager who is not the subject of the grievance. This should be done in writing and should set out the nature of the grievance."

There is no benefit in arguing that an employee has not raised a formal grievance just because it has not been expressed as such. If the employee has made a complaint, then it should be addressed, regardless of how it has been categorised.

However, the Code of Practice does state that the grievance should be in writing. This can be helpful. Not only does it mean that there is a record of the grievance, but asking the employee to put everything down in writing helps the employee to organise their thoughts and make sure they have not missed out any important information. It also helps the employer to make sure all of the points are investigated and responded to.

You need to select who will conduct the grievance process. This will often be the employee's line manager, or possibly somebody one level up but with whom the employee does not have regular contact. The grievance officer (as they are inelegantly known) should not be the most senior person in the company, as you need to keep someone back to conduct an appeal, should one be required. Sometimes – particularly if the grievance is against the CEO or someone from HR, or if you do not have the time or expertise to deal with the grievance internally – you should consider appointing an external person to conduct the grievance process. See more about selecting and appointing an external person in Appendix 2.

As soon as the employee has raised their grievance, you should acknowledge it. First, meet with them to confirm receipt of the grievance and to ask them any questions necessary to enable you to understand the grievance sufficiently to carry out the investigation. This is not a formal grievance meeting, so there is no legal requirement to allow the employee to be accompanied. However, if the employee does ask to be accompanied by a colleague or a trade union representative, you should allow them to do so. If the employee has a disability of any kind, it is often a good idea to exercise discretion to allow them to be accompanied by a friend or family member who really understands how to help them cope with the disability and put their points across in what might seem to be a very formal setting.

In addition to meeting with the employee, write to them to confirm receipt of the grievance and to set out what you plan to do next. The letter should include a summary of what you discussed with the employee when you met. You do not need to provide a detailed plan of the investigation, but you need to give the employee some idea of how long they will have to wait for a grievance meeting, and what you will be doing in the meantime. For example:

"I anticipate that it will be about three weeks before I will be able to arrange the formal grievance meeting. This is because I want to interview four employees to investigate the points that you have raised, and one of them is on holiday next week."

If the issues are complex and are going to take some time to investigate, and/or if the issue is particularly upsetting, it is good practice to schedule an additional 'catch-up' meeting with the employee.

For example:

> "As I explained to you when we met, it is going to take me at least three weeks to investigate the points that you raised. That is because I am on annual leave next week, and I need to interview a number of employees to explore the issues. I do appreciate that you were upset when we met, and so I would like to arrange a meeting to catch up with you as soon as I am back from leave. This is not a grievance meeting, but just an informal opportunity to check on your wellbeing."

If the employee is particularly upset, it would be useful to direct the employee to an employee assistance programme, if your organisation has one. Alternatively, make sure that the employee is aware of external support organisations (e.g. the Samaritans).

You do sometimes need to be flexible. Rigid adherence to the strict wording of a policy can trigger criticism, just as departure from the policy can do. Ultimately, you might need to persuade a tribunal you've acted reasonably, so don't stick slavishly to the wording of a policy if it's unreasonable to do so.

GMB Trade Union v Brown (2007) UKEAT/0621/06

The employee's manager proposed changes to her job. The company grievance procedure required her to raise her grievance with her manager before moving to the next stage of the procedure. She had four unproductive meetings with her manager, which did not conclude the grievance, so she asked to skip this stage because further meetings would make her ill. When this request was refused, she went off sick with stress and later resigned. She successfully claimed constructive dismissal, arguing that her employer had breached the implied term of mutual trust and confidence by failing to deal with her grievance and failing to be flexible about the grievance policy.

CHECKLIST

Ask the employee to confirm the grievance in writing, so that you are sure that you have understood every aspect of the issue.	
Write to the employee to confirm receipt of the grievance, and to outline the timescales prior to arranging a formal grievance meeting.	
Meet with the employee to confirm receipt of the grievance, and to seek any further clarification. (Also, if the employee is disabled, discuss whether any adjustments will be needed during the process.)	
Consider whether you are the appropriate person to manage the grievance process. If not you, who?	
Direct the employee to an appropriate support service if necessary.	
Depending on the complaint, ask the employee for details of any person who can assist in the investigation.	

CHAPTER 4

The grievance investigation

The issues raised in the grievance need to be investigated. This is crucial even if the issues seem straightforward. This is because:

- it is only through investigation that you can be certain that you have fully understood the issues.

- you might think that you know what is happening, but you might be wrong.

- you need to try to understand the issue from the employee's perspective, and a thorough investigation will enable you to do this.

You need to start by planning out the investigation. Use this checklist to help you plan:

CHECKLIST

What are the issues raised in the grievance? (List them all in summary format.)	
For each issue – who would have more information? (Think about who might have seen something happen, who might have been present at a conversation, and who might know the policies and procedures being referred to. List them for each of the issues). These are the people that you need to interview.	
Are there any documents (e.g. policies, timesheets, quality records) that would help you investigate the issues raised? (List relevant documents for each issue.)	

Then, from this, develop an action plan to explore the grievance. For example:

Action	What to find out	Responsibility	Deadline
Interview Barry	Did he hear Fred swear at Raj on 4 April? Has he ever heard Fred and Raj arguing?	Me	31 May
Review timesheets	Was Raj late to work on 4 April?	Me	27 May
Review the policy	Has there been a breach of the policy?	Me/HR	1 April

Then, once you have planned out what you need to do, go and do it.

Remember that some people who are the subject of the grievance (e.g. a manager accused of bullying) might be motivated to 'even the score' by telling their exaggerated versions of the truth. They position themselves as the most caring, the most approachable, the most 'saintly' manager that you're ever likely to meet. The investigation can be like a negotiation, with both sides starting at opposite extremes. The aim of the grievance investigation is to identify the truth that lies somewhere in the middle.

It is highly likely that there will be some element of the grievance which requires you to interview witnesses. If you do need to interview a witness, follow these steps:

Interview step 1: Invite the witness to an investigation meeting

You need to ask the witness to meet with you. Occasionally, you might decide that you do not want to give the witness any notice of the meeting because you want the witness to give an immediate response to your questions rather than giving you a response that has been carefully prepared. But that should be unusual. More commonly, you'll want the witness to gather together pieces of evidence in advance, or have a chance to think, recall and structure their thoughts, and you'll need to give sufficient notice to allow for this.

The witness does not have a legal right to be accompanied by a union representative or workplace colleague (as the person bringing the grievance does). But if they want to be accompanied, especially if they are nervous or have a disability, it's sensible to agree. Just make it clear that the person accompanying the witness is not there to answer questions; they're just there to provide moral support.

When you invite the witness to the meeting, think about what they need to know. It might be necessary to say that someone has raised a grievance, and to set out the nature of the grievance. But sometimes you may need to be more vague, especially if sensitive issues arise.

Unless it is really essential, or will be obvious in any event, do not identify the employee who has raised the grievance. If it is essential (or obvious), make sure that the employee who raised the grievance is aware that this is going to happen. You can instruct the witness to keep the invitation to the meeting, the meeting itself, and all issues associated with the meeting confidential, and warn them that breaching confidence will be a disciplinary matter for themselves.

SAMPLE INVITATION LETTER:

Dear [name of witness]

I have received a grievance from a member of staff which I am in the process of looking into. I would like you to come to a meeting at [time] on [date] at [place] to discuss [summarise the issues, giving the witness sufficient details to be able to prepare]. It would be very helpful if you could bring [list any documents, or other materials that might be helpful] with you.

The purpose of the meeting is for me to understand the issues more fully. You are not suspected of any wrongdoing. I am simply investigating the facts so that I can respond to the grievance.

You are required to keep this request for a meeting, and anything we discuss at the meeting, confidential.

If the date and time proposed for the meeting are not convenient, or if you have any questions, please let me know.

Yours sincerely
[Name and job title]

Interview step 2: Preparation for the investigation meeting

Once you have invited the witness to the meeting, you need to prepare. Go back to the issues that you are investigating and identify the questions that need to be answered.

When probing the complex issues, you should try to use open questions to make sure that the witness is giving an accurate account (and not feeling pressured to say what they think you want them to say). Use words such as:

How?

Why?

When?

Where?

What?

Prepare your questions, but also be ready to deviate from them. You do not know what the witness is going to say, and they might raise very important points that you do not yet know about.

Interview step 3: At the investigation meeting

The purpose of the investigation meeting is to gather facts about the situation that will determine how you address the grievance. It is necessary, therefore, to make thorough notes at the meeting. If you are not the person who manages the formal grievance meeting these notes will be crucial for the person who does. The notes could also be useful for a manager who hears a subsequent appeal. It is not always easy to listen to answers, consider them, and frame the follow-up question at the same time as writing everything down. It is therefore usually better to have an independent note-taker present or, subject to consent, digitally record the meeting.

In larger organisations, the notes may be typed up into a statement which the witness should be asked to check, review if necessary, and sign. But for most businesses, this is too formal and is not necessary for a grievance process (unlike for a disciplinary process, where it is more common).

Of course, every situation is different, and it is not possible to write one detailed script that will cover all aspects of the investigation meeting. However, the following points are a useful checklist of what to cover at the meeting.

CHECKLIST

Thank the witness for attending and (if not known to each other) carry out introductions.	
Introduce the note-taker and explain their role (or explain the digital recording process if consent is given).	
If the witness attends with a representative, tell the witness that it is not a formal meeting, and that they therefore have no right to have a representative present. Decide whether you will allow the representative to stay or ask them to leave. (Usually, it's best to allow the representative to stay, unless there's a good reason that they should not.)	
Summarise the purpose of the meeting.	

Explain to the witness how the information they share will be used. In particular, make it clear whether the information will be shared with the employee who has raised the grievance, or the person against whom the grievance has been raised.	
Ask the witness your questions.	
Ask the witness to talk you through any documents or other materials they have brought to the meeting.	
Ask the witness if they have any questions for you.	
Explain what will happen next (you will type the information into a formal statement, and they can review and correct anything before signing it).	
Remind the witness that the process is confidential, and that it should remain confidential.	
Thank the witness for attending.	

Interview step 4: Questions from the employee who presented the grievance

The employee who raised the grievance may disagree with some of the witness's account. To make sure the hearing is fair, they need to be told the gist of that account – unless there is a very compelling reason not to do so. There are normally two ways to do that:

a. show the employee who raised the grievance your notes from the investigation meeting (or any formal statement). That is best practice, although it might involve you having to type up your notes so they are legible (see top tip, below).

b. summarise the witnesses account for the employee raising the grievance. This is a less desirable approach, as if they end up in litigation with you, they will seize on any discrepancy or omission in your summary as evidence of an unfair procedure or bad faith.

TOP TIP: Very few people have the time or inclination to type up notes. One way to avoid that is to digitally record the meetings and then use a digital transcription service to type them up. I recommend rev.com for digital transcript; at the time of writing, they charge $1.25 for each minute of recording, so a one-hour meeting costs $75, or about £60, to transcribe. Best of all, you get the transcript back within 24 hours. If you use the link bit.ly/hric-rev, I get a small commission and it doesn't cost you any more, so please have a think about using that link instead.

If the employee raising the grievance sees the statement and disagrees with it (in a material way, rather than disagreeing with some background narrative, which is less important), there are three ways to deal with it:

a. hold a further meeting at which either you – or the employee raising the grievance – asks further questions of the witness. Although the employee raising the grievance will often want to confront the witness directly, it is unusual to allow them to do so and there is no legal requirement for you to allow it. If you want to allow it, you could invite the witness to attend the actual grievance meeting to answer questions, which reduces the number of extra meetings you have to arrange.

b. ask the employee raising the grievance to put some questions in an email for you to pass on to the witness, and them forward them to the witness for an answer.

Problem area: what if the witness is uncooperative?

What do you do if someone has been identified as a witness, but they do not want to get involved?

Firstly, think about how important the witness's evidence is to understanding the grievance. If it is not crucial, it is probably easiest to exclude the witness from the process.

However, be aware that excluding one witness could lead to someone else who was willing to be a witness opting to withdraw. Being a witness is not an experience that many people relish, and if others know that there is an opportunity to refuse, it could make the investigation very difficult.

If you conclude that the witness's evidence is likely to be crucial, then try the following steps:

a. meet with the witness informally to talk about the process. Establish why they want to avoid being a witness. Can you reassure them about their concerns?

b. when you meet with the witness, explain why their evidence is important and how it is going to be used. Make it clear why their contribution is so valuable.

c. reassure them that they will not have to be questioned face to face by the employee, and that your organisation will not allow repercussions from others for being a witness.

Another option is to assure the witness of anonymity. Before doing this, you need to consider whether it is really possible for a witness to be anonymous. Will who has said what be obvious to the employee who raised the grievance just from the content of the statement? Simply redacting the name of the witness may not be sufficient to protect their anonymity. If they were the only other witness to an event, conversation or incident, the inclusion of any details relating to this would identify them and would therefore also need to excluded from the investigation report.

You also need to balance the rights of the employee who raised the grievance to have the opportunity to challenge anything that is said, against the rights of the witness not to face any difficulties as a result of giving evidence.

Ultimately, remember this: you are the boss, not the employee who you are asking to be a witness. Giving an account of events in a meeting is part and parcel of the employment relationship, and it is a reasonable and lawful instruction. You are entitled to treat a refusal to cooperate as a disciplinary matter, should you wish to do so.

Witnesses outside the organisation

Sometimes, someone outside your organisation will be a key witness. This could be a customer, a supplier, or even a passer-by. Clearly, it is more difficult to get someone external to be a witness, but it might be necessary.

Before deciding to use an external witness, you should think about the commercial implications. For example, do you want a key customer to be drawn into internal employee tensions? Probably not.

Remember that external witnesses may be harder to control when it comes to confidentiality.

CHAPTER 5

The grievance meeting

Paragraphs 33 and 34 of the Code of Practice state:

33. Employers should arrange for a formal meeting to be held without unreasonable delay after a grievance is received.

34. Employers, employees and their companions should make every effort to attend the meeting. Employees should be allowed to explain their grievance and how they think it should be resolved. Consideration should be given to adjourning the meeting for any investigation that may be necessary.

The employee should be invited to the grievance meeting by letter.

SAMPLE LETTER

Dear [name of employee]

I am writing in response to the grievance that you raised with me on [date]. We had an informal chat about this on [date] and since then I have been carrying out some investigations so that I could meet with you and discuss the matter in more detail. This meeting will be on [date] at [time] at [place].

As this is a formal grievance meeting, you are entitled to be accompanied by a colleague or trade union representative. You do not have to be accompanied by a representative; if you prefer, you can come alone. If you choose to be accompanied by a representative, please let me know their name before the meeting.

[[Name and job title] will also be at the meeting to take notes.] [The meeting will be recorded and we will provide you with a copy of the recording, and the transcript if we transcribe it, afterwards.]

[You may make your own recording of the meeting if you wish to do so, but please tell us if you intend to do so.] [We do not normally allow the meetings to be recorded, so please do not attempt to do so. If you covertly record the meeting, it may be regarded as a serious disciplinary issue and may affect how we assess your integrity if there are any disputed issues. Your representative, or you, can take notes in the meeting as it progresses.]

At the meeting, I will ask you questions about your grievance, and I will also present to you the findings of my investigations so far. There will be a chance for you to give me more details about your grievance, to respond to the evidence I have collected, and to ask questions.

At the end of the meeting, it might be necessary for me to adjourn, to carry out further investigations. If this is necessary, I will explain to you what I plan to do and the likely timescale involved.

If you and/or your representative are unable to attend the meeting, please let me know as soon as possible so that I can make alternative arrangements. If you have any questions at all please do not hesitate to contact me.

Yours sincerely
[Name and job title]

At the meeting

It is traditional to hold the grievance meeting face to face, but it's absolutely fine to hold it another way if there is a good reason to do so (such as a manager who works during the day dealing with a grievance from a night-shift worker, where that worker might not be able to come into the office during the day, or an employee who is unwell or – at the time of writing this book – because employees are shielding due to coronavirus).

Various alternatives to face-to-face meetings include holding the meeting over Zoom or Skype, or even by telephone if the employee lacks the technology for Zoom or Skype. It is also common to hold the meetings in a neutral venue, such as a hotel, if there is a good reason for the employee to not come into the workplace. Short of that, it is not unheard of for employees to decline to attend a face-to-face meeting and instead send in written representations.

Ahead of the grievance meeting, make sure that you have all the practical arrangements in place (i.e. that no-one will disturb the meeting, your phone is switched off, and your email alerts are turned off). It is useful to have a jug of water and some glasses, as they are useful props for thinking time, and also helpful if the employee becomes emotional. Having some tissues in the room somewhere discreet is also useful.

During the meeting, listen carefully, ask questions to clarify points, and be aware of things like your tone and body language. In terms of resolving workplace conflict, the manner in which a grievance is considered by management can often be just as important as the final decision itself. If the employee feels that their complaints have been treated seriously and respectfully, they are much less likely to bear a grudge or bring a tribunal claim.

Work through this checklist at the meeting:

CHECKLIST

Thank the employee (and, if they are accompanied, their representative) for attending. Make introductions.	
Introduce the note-taker and explain their role or, if you're recording the meeting, tell the employee you are doing so (after you've started the recording). If you are not recording the meeting, ask them to confirm they are not making a recording of the meeting or, alternatively, ask them to make their recording openly and not covertly.	

If the employee is not accompanied, ask the employee if they understand that they are entitled to have a representative and confirm whether they have chosen to come alone. Make sure that this response is noted or recorded.	
Summarise the purpose of the meeting.	
Choose whether to sum up the grievance as you understand it, or whether to ask the employee to summarise the grievance. If the employee seems nervous, it's generally sensible for you to do the summary and then ask the employee to correct you if you have got anything wrong or missed anything out.	
Ask the employee if they have any questions.	
Present the findings of your investigation to date.	
Ask the employee any questions of clarification.	
Ask the employee if there is anything else they would like to tell you, or if they have any further questions.	
Summarise your understanding of all that has been said.	
Explain to the employee that you are going to adjourn to think about all that has been said, and to decide the next steps/outcome. Give some indication of how long the adjournment will be.	
Adjourn the meeting.	

When you reconvene, explain to the employee what you have concluded. If you have decided that further investigation is needed, give a suggested timescale.	
If no further investigation is needed, explain your decision on how the grievance will be addressed.	
Inform the employee that the decision will be confirmed in writing.	
Inform the employee that they can appeal if they are not happy with your decision.	

Managing witnesses

Depending upon your grievance policy, you may allow witnesses to attend the investigation meeting for the employee to question. Witnesses should only join the meeting to answer questions; they should not then be present for the remainder of the meeting.

It is important to keep tight control of the questioning of witnesses, so that the process does not turn into an argument. Work through this checklist for each witness:

CHECKLIST

Thank the witness for attending. Make introductions.	
Advise the employee and the witness that the employee can only ask the witness for points of clarification.	
Ask the employee to ask the first question.	
Invite the witness to respond.	
Allow this process of question and response to continue. Intervene if any question seems inappropriate.	
When the employee has asked all of their questions, consider whether you have any questions to ask.	
Thank the witness for their attendance, and remind them of the importance of keeping the proceedings confidential.	

CHAPTER 6

The right to be accompanied

The Code of Practice covers the right to be accompanied at a formal discipline or grievance hearing. From a legal perspective, the right to be accompanied is contained in the Employment Relations Act 1999.

The Code of Practice states:

35. Workers have a statutory right to be accompanied by a companion at a grievance meeting which deals with a complaint about a duty owed by the employer to the worker. So this would apply where the complaint is, for example, that the employer is not honouring the worker's contract, or is in breach of legislation.

36. The statutory right is to be accompanied by a fellow worker, a trade union representative, or an official employed by a trade union. A trade union representative who is not an employed official must have been certified by their union as being competent to accompany a worker. Employers must agree to a worker's request to be accompanied by any companion from one of these categories. Workers may also alter their choice of companion if they wish. As a matter of good practice, in making their choice workers should bear in mind the practicalities of the arrangements. For instance, a worker may choose to be accompanied by a companion who is suitable, willing and available on site rather than someone from a geographically remote location.

There will often be circumstances where it would be wise to allow an employee to be accompanied by someone other than a colleague or trade union representative. For example:

- if an employee is disabled and that disability might impede their ability to understand the proceedings (e.g. a learning disability), it would normally be appropriate – and probably required as a reasonable adjustment under the Equality Act 2020 – to allow the employee to be accompanied by a carer who understands the employee's specific needs.

- if an employee is aged under 18 years, it might be appropriate to allow the employee to be accompanied by a parent or carer, given that they are not an adult.

- if an employee does not speak English as their first language, it might be appropriate to allow the employee to be accompanied by someone who can translate for them (this could be in addition to the representative if the translator is only going to translate, and not carry out the representation role).

My view is that it is often sensible to allow the employee to be accompanied by whomever they choose (with two exceptions, below). Often, a trusted advisor (whether a friend or relative) can provide an objective assessment of your response to the employee's case, or can talk the employee down from taking things further or bringing tribunal proceedings. The employee is more likely to trust their friend or relative's assessment than that of a union rep or workplace colleague, whom they might not think is entirely 'on their side'.

There are two exceptions to that. First, it is unwise to allow the employee to be accompanied by a lawyer. A lawyer's purpose will usually be to disrupt and trigger exchanges that could be used in a tribunal. The employee has no right to legal representation, unless the meeting could mean the end of their career (as may be the case for a doctor or nurse, a city trader, or a teacher). In reality, this is going to be rare in a grievance scenario.

Second, it is perfectly reasonable to refuse to allow a family member to attend if they are combative or belligerent. If somebody becomes combative during a meeting, the best way to deal with it is to take a 10-minute break and, if they continue, warn them that you will ask them to leave. If you end up asking them to leave, and they do not, you are perfectly at liberty to suspend the meeting and tell the employee it will be concluded on another date, without their family member present. Note that because of the case below (Toal), you cannot take this approach if the employee raising the grievance is accompanied by a combative workplace colleague or trade union representative.

Having said that, many HR professionals read the legislation restrictively, and argue that because the Employment Relations Act 1999 states that an employee has the right to be accompanied by a workplace colleague or union representative, it follows that they cannot be accompanied by anyone else. For the reasons above, this approach carries risk; the overarching obligation on an employer is to act reasonably.

I deal with this issue in more detail in my video 'How to Handle Disciplinary, Dismissal and

Performance Management Situations', starting at 37:55. You can watch the video (and subscribe to my YouTube channel) at bit.ly/dismissalvideo.

Paragraph 37 of the Code of Practice states:

37. To exercise the statutory right to be accompanied, workers must make a reasonable request. What is reasonable will depend on the circumstances of each individual case. A request to be accompanied does not have to be in writing or within a certain time frame. However, a worker should provide enough time for the employer to deal with the companion's attendance at the meeting. Workers should also consider how they make their request so that it is clearly understood, for instance by letting the employer know in advance the name of the companion where possible and whether they are a fellow worker or trade union official or representative.

This paragraph starts by referring to the employee making a 'reasonable request' to be accompanied. This could be read as meaning that the employer can decide who a reasonable representative might be. However, that is not so. If the employee chooses to be represented by a colleague or a trade union representative, an employer cannot argue and say that a different representative should be chosen. If the employee chooses someone who is perceived as a troublemaker, and you would really like them to choose someone else, unfortunately you do not have the right to choose.

> ### Toal v GB Oils Ltd (2013) IRLR 696
>
> The claimant was attending a grievance meeting, and his employer refused to allow him to be accompanied by his chosen representative, a trade union official (the case report does not say why, but I infer that the employer thought the union official was 'difficult'). As a result, the employee chose someone else to accompany him.
>
> He brought a claim that he had been denied his right to be accompanied at a formal grievance meeting by a representative of his choice, and the Employment Appeal Tribunal upheld his claim. The employee had chosen a trade union representative, which was allowed by law. Although the Code of Practice refers to making a 'reasonable' request, it is not for the employer to choose who is reasonable.
>
> The employee was awarded a nominal sum of compensation, in the order of £2.

As we can see, paragraph 37 states that the employee should ideally let their employer know in advance of the meeting who their representative will be, and explain the reason that the representative is allowed to accompany the employee (simply to say whether they are a colleague or trade union representative).

In practical terms, it is a good idea to ask the employee who is going to accompany them in the letter arranging the grievance meeting. This allows you to know who is going to be away from their work and attending the meeting, so that you can provide appropriate cover.

Paragraph 38 of the Code of Practice states:

38. If a worker's chosen companion will not be available at the time proposed for the hearing by the employer, the employer must postpone the hearing to a time proposed by the worker provided that the alternative time is both reasonable and not more than five working days after the date originally proposed.

This reflects the legal position in the Employment Relations Act 1999, and it requires you to adjourn a grievance hearing for up to five working days to enable a chosen companion to attend if the employee proposes an alternative date within those five working days. This can cause immense frustration for employers when managing grievance hearings. You have carried out your initial investigations, you've arranged a date which everyone else can make – but the chosen representative is not available.

If the representative is not available at any time within five working days of the date originally proposed then, under the strict reading of the Employment Relations Act 1999, you could go ahead with your chosen time. However, if the representative is available shortly after the five working days, then insisting on going ahead could be considered unreasonable. Again, to illustrate this, I turn to a case relating to a disciplinary situation:

Talon Engineering Ltd v Smith (2018) IRLR 1104

Mrs Smith sent an email to a customer. The email included insulting language. She was suspended on 29 July and invited to a disciplinary hearing to take place on 5 September. The hearing was postponed due to ill health and annual leave, and rescheduled for 29 September.

Mrs Smith's union representative was not available on 29 September but was available on another date that was just under two weeks later. The request to wait for the representative was refused because the representative was not available at a time within five working days

---

of the rescheduled date for the hearing. Mrs Smith refused to attend the meeting without her representative. The meeting went ahead in her absence and she was dismissed.

This was found to be an unfair dismissal because it was procedurally unfair due to not waiting those extra few days for the representative. The Employment Appeal Tribunal noted that the Employment Relations Act 1999 only gave an absolute right to postpone for up to five working days, but under general unfair dismissal law, the employer still had to act reasonably – and it was not reasonable to refuse to postpone for an extra week or so beyond the five working days.

It is all about being reasonable. The Employment Relations Act 1999 might only require you to wait for five working days, but overall, there is a requirement to act reasonably. There is not a requirement to rearrange a hearing for weeks ahead, but allowing an extra few days is likely to be a reasonable request.

Paragraph 39 of the Code of Practice states:

39. The companion should be allowed to address the hearing to put and sum up the worker's case, respond on behalf of the worker to any views expressed at the meeting and confer with the worker during the hearing. The companion does not, however, have the right to answer questions on the worker's behalf, address the hearing if the worker does not wish it or prevent the employer from explaining their case.

In a grievance hearing you want to hear what the employee has to say. You want their explanation of the issues, and their evidence. However, there are times when the employee is very upset and unable to explain what they want to say, or when the employee is very nervous and struggles to talk clearly. There could also be the situation in which the employee just cannot express themselves clearly for other reasons.

In that situation, it is useful to have a representative to talk on behalf of the employee, providing that the representative understands the employee's grievance. If the representative is speaking for the employee you can still turn to the employee and ask simple questions, such as:

Has your representative explained your grievance correctly?

Is there anything that you want to add to what your representative has said?

If the representative seems to be giving their own interpretation of the issues or is talking over the employee, or is otherwise disrupting the hearing, you can ask the representative to be quiet and say that you want the employee to answer the next question. In addition, the employee can ask their representative to be quiet and allow them to speak if they wish to do so.

The right to representation only applies to formal disciplinary and grievance meetings. However, refusing to allow an employee to be represented at an informal meeting could potentially be a breach of the implied term of mutual trust and confidence.

Saint Francis Hospice v Burn (2013) UKEAT/0486/12

An employee had been absent due to illness for a long time. Whilst absent, she had raised a number of grievances which, in summary, were allegations of harassment and bullying by management. She was invited to a meeting with management to discuss this informally, but was refused the right to be accompanied.

She resigned and successfully claimed constructive dismissal, arguing that the implied term of mutual trust and confidence had been breached. Although this was not a formal grievance meeting, not allowing her to be accompanied, given the distress that she was in, amounted to a breach.

CHAPTER 7
The decision

The Code of Practice states:

40. Following the meeting, decide on what action, if any, to take. Decisions should be communicated to the employee, in writing, without unreasonable delay and, where appropriate, should set out what action the employer intends to take to resolve the grievance. The employee should be informed that they can appeal if they are not content with the action taken.

It sounds obvious, but if a grievance is raised, then an employer should try to find a solution. Listening to the complaint and then saying that 'nothing can be done' without really trying to find a solution is not meeting the obligations of an employer.

Waltons & Morse v Dorrington (1997) IRLR 488

Mrs Dorrington worked in an open-plan area, and some colleagues she worked with smoked (this was in the days before smoking in enclosed spaces was banned). She complained, following which smoking was banned in open-plan areas, but employees with their own offices could still smoke in them. In addition, a smoking area was designated – right by Mrs Dorrington's work station. She asked to move and this was refused, so she moved anyway and was told to move back. She resigned and successfully claimed constructive dismissal.

The Employment Appeal Tribunal held that her grievance had not been properly addressed. The employer should have tried to find a solution.

It is always a good idea to ask the employee what they want. Ideally, they should tell you what they're looking for in their grievance letter (although few employees actually do that). During the grievance meeting, it is quite appropriate to ask them what they actually want you to do (and to ask that as many times as you need, until you get an answer). Sometimes, they will say that they don't actually know what they want you to do, or that they don't think there is anything you can do, which makes it easier to defend any future claim they might bring on the basis you failed to resolve the grievance properly.

After you have attended the grievance meeting and completed any additional investigations, work through the following questions:

CHECKLIST

What was the original grievance? (It might help to write this down.)	
Now that all of the evidence has been gathered, has the grievance been refined/altered in any way? (Again, writing this down can be useful.)	
What evidence have you found that supports this grievance? (Make a list.)	
What evidence have you found that does not support the grievance? (Make a list.)	
Based on your analysis, is there a grievance to address or does your evidence suggest that the grievance is not well founded?	
If the grievance is not well founded, how will you explain this to the employee whilst still being supportive? (Write out the words you will use.)	
If the grievance is well founded, what can you do to address this? (Set out an action plan.)	

You will need to communicate your decision to the employee. You should arrange to meet with the employee to explain your conclusions and your decision. As this is still part of the formal grievance process, you should allow your employee to attend the meeting with their representative. This can be a nerve-wracking part of the process for a manager, especially if the employee is likely to be unhappy with the decision, and you may want to prepare, or even confidentially rehearse, feedback to be given beforehand so you feel more confident in the meeting itself. Needless to say, decisions should be explained respectfully and openly, whatever they are.

You should confirm the outcome in writing. This outcome letter is an important document, as if the employee brings (say) constructive dismissal or discrimination proceedings, it is the document on which a tribunal will place the most weight, and it will be subject to the most scrutiny.

There might be some actions that you are not able to share with the employee. For example, if the employee has raised a grievance that they are being bullied and your investigations support the allegation, then you might conclude that you need to take disciplinary action against the bully. You should tell the employee that you are putting the other employee through a formal disciplinary process, but you should not share the details of those proceedings, as they are confidential to the other employee.

Your letter should state that the employee has the right to appeal against your decision:

SAMPLE LETTER

Dear [name of employee]

I am writing in response to your grievance which you set out in writing on [date]. We subsequently met on [list all dates of meetings]. I was accompanied at the meetings by [name and job title]. [You chose not to be accompanied by a representative] or [You were accompanied at the meetings by [name and job title]].

I have given careful consideration to everything that you raised, and the information I gathered in my investigation.

[Set out the steps you took, the evidence that supports or undermines the grievance, and explain why you have reached your conclusion. This section could be just a couple of paragraphs, or it might be several pages, depending on the complexity of the grievance.]

[If the grievance is accepted partially or in full] We will be taking the following action to address the points you raised: [outline the action to be taken]

[If the grievance is not accepted in full] If you are dissatisfied with the outcome of this grievance, you are entitled to appeal. Appeals should be sent within five working days of receipt of this letter. Any appeal should be addressed to [name, job title and contact details].

I hope that you feel your grievance has been fully addressed and that you are satisfied with my response.

Yours sincerely

[Name and job title]

YES SIR, I FINISHED THE GRIEVANCE REPORT TWO DAYS AGO - I'M JUST TRYING TO DECIDE WHICH FONT TO USE.

DANIEL BARNETT

CHAPTER 8

Appeals

The Code of Practice states:

41. Where an employee feels that their grievance has not been satisfactorily resolved they should appeal. They should let their employer know the grounds for their appeal without unreasonable delay and in writing.

42. Appeals should be heard without unreasonable delay and at a time and place which should be notified to the employee in advance.

43. The appeal should be dealt with impartially and wherever possible by a manager who has not previously been involved in the case.

44. Workers have a statutory right to be accompanied at any such appeal hearing.

45. The outcome of the appeal should be communicated to the employee in writing without unreasonable delay.

The appeal process is broadly similar to the original grievance hearing:

- the process should start with the employee putting their concerns (i.e. their grounds for appeal) in writing.

- the appeal hearing should be held promptly.

- the employee should be given adequate notice of the appeal hearing.

- the employee is entitled to be accompanied at the appeal hearing.

- the outcome of the appeal hearing should be communicated in writing.

The first step in managing an appeal is deciding who should hear it. Ideally, this should be a manager who is senior to the person who conducted the original grievance process (because someone who is junior or at the same level might find it more difficult to disagree with a decision). In addition, it is preferable that the manager considering the appeal has not been involved in any discussions about the grievance to date and, ideally, knows nothing about it.

In a large organisation this is not usually too difficult. There are typically a number of managers to choose from, and ideally someone from a different part of the business will hear the appeal.

In a small organisation it is less likely to be possible to find someone who knows nothing about the grievance. An employment tribunal will accept this but would expect you to do the best that you can. Is there a manager who knows very little about what has happened? Maybe a manager who was on leave when the issues were first raised? It might be helpful to ask someone outside the organisation to hear the appeal. For example, some small businesses are part of a local network and managers from one business will hear appeals at another, and vice versa.

Sometimes, if your organisation lacks the resources to deal with the appeal, it can be useful to outsource it – see Appendix 2. It is important that the appeal officer is independent and is willing to overturn a decision if they think it is wrong or unreasonable. Some managers shy away from doing so as they think it shows weakness or undermines the manager who made the first decision. I (in common with all experienced lawyers) have cross-examined many dozens of appeal officers who simply 'rubber-stamped' a grievance or disciplinary decision. In a tribunal, it is <u>much</u> easier than you would think to demonstrate an appeal officer has not applied sufficient scrutiny and rigour to the appeal process, and make the appeal officer look incompetent or worse. Having an external person conduct the appeal does not eliminate the problem, but it does reduce the risk.

Blackburn v Aldi Stores Ltd (2013) IRLR 846

The employee raised a grievance and, following a grievance hearing, the complaints were dismissed. The employee appealed. The appeal was held by the same manager who heard the original grievance and (not surprisingly) the appeal was dismissed.

The employee resigned and successfully claimed constructive dismissal. Addressing the appeal in this way meant that the procedure had not been followed fairly and this was a breach of mutual trust and confidence.

Once the person deciding the appeal has been identified, they need to be provided with all of the materials gathered to date. They then need to meet with the employee to understand the basis for the appeal. It might be that the employee has new evidence that they want to present. It might be that the employee thinks that the manager hearing the grievance misunderstood something important.

What is important is to understand the grounds for the appeal.

SAMPLE LETTER

Dear [name of employee]

I am writing in response to the appeal that you have raised in writing on [date] against the outcome of your grievance meeting.

I would like to invite you to a meeting to formally discuss your appeal. This will be on [date] at [time] at [place].

You are entitled to be accompanied by a colleague or trade union representative. You do not have to be accompanied by a representative; if you prefer, you can come alone. If you choose to be accompanied by a representative, please let me know their name before the meeting.

I will be accompanied at the meeting by [name and job title]. [Name and job title] will also be present to take notes. They will not be involved in any discussions or decisions about the grievance; their role is just to take the notes. [Alternatively a paragraph about recording the meeting].

At this meeting, I would like to understand the grounds for your appeal against the original outcome of the grievance. Please come to the meeting prepared to explain this to me. Additionally, if you are planning on submitting any new evidence, then please bring this with you to the meeting.

At the end of the meeting, it might be necessary for me to adjourn, to carry out further investigations. If this is necessary, I will explain to you what investigations I plan to carry out and tell you about the likely timescales involved.

If you, or your representative, are unable to attend the meeting, please let me know as soon as possible so that I can make alternative arrangements. If you have any questions at all, please do not hesitate to contact me.

Yours sincerely

[Name and job title]

At the appeal hearing, the manager chairing/ considering the appeal should explain the purpose of the meeting, and then invite the employee to explain the basis of their appeal:

CHECKLIST

Thank the employee and their representative for attending. Make introductions (including introducing any note-taker and explaining their role).	
If the employee arrives without a representative, ask the employee if they understand that they are entitled to have a representative, and confirm whether they have chosen to come alone. Make sure that this response is noted or recorded.	
Summarise the purpose of the meeting.	
Explain to the employee that you have read the papers relating to the grievance, and would like to understand the basis for the appeal. Ask the employee to explain.	
Ask the employee any questions of clarification.	
Sum up your understanding of all that has been said.	
Explain to the employee that you are going to adjourn to consider all that has been said and to decide what needs to be done. Give some indication of how the adjournment is likely to be.	
Adjourn the meeting.	

When you reconvene, explain to the employee what you have concluded. If you have decided that further investigations are needed, give a suggested timescale.	
If no further investigations are needed, explain your decision on the appeal.	
Inform the employee that the decision will be confirmed in writing.	

If new evidence is brought to the appeal hearing, it is almost inevitable that the meeting will need to be adjourned to allow the manager deciding the appeal time to consider that evidence. It might be possible to address this in a short adjournment and then to reconvene the hearing, or there might be a need to interview new witnesses, meaning that the hearing will need to be adjourned for a number of days.

The appeal meeting is a very important part of the process. If there were flaws in the way that the grievance hearing was managed, the appeal meeting can sometimes be used to rectify those flaws.

CHAPTER 9

After the process has ended

Hopefully, once the grievance process (including appeal, where applicable) has finished, the situation will be resolved. However, there are still some points that need to be considered:

Monitoring the situation

If you have decided to take some action, as a result of the grievance being upheld, it needs to be monitored. Is the action having the desired impact? It will often be sensible to arrange a time for a follow-up meeting with the employee so that you can check that the employee is happy that the situation is resolved.

If you have decided not to take any action, you might still want to keep a check on the situation. It might be worth checking, after an appropriate time, that the situation has not escalated such that action is now needed.

Taking disciplinary action against the person causing the grievance

Sometimes, the outcome of the grievance will be that you need to take disciplinary action against the person who was accused of wrongdoing. The decision whether to do this will depend on the specific situation. There is no requirement to take disciplinary action or dismiss because the employee raising the grievance wishes you to do so, or suggests that it should happen.

Barratt v Accrington &Rossendale College (2006) UKEAT/0099/66

The employee raising the grievance had been assaulted by a colleague. He resigned and claimed constructive dismissal arguing that there was a breach of the implied term of mutual trust and confidence when the employer decided not to dismiss the colleague.

The claim failed. The employer had taken into account the colleague's unblemished record and had reasonably concluded that it was not fair to dismiss.

If you decide to invoke a disciplinary process, you will need to make sure you follow the correct procedures. This will be the subject of a future book. For now, it is best to start by referring to the Code of Practice and, if you do not have an internal HR person, finding an independent HR professional to advise you. You can use my list of those experienced in investigations, at bit.ly/grievanceinvestigations.

CHAPTER 10

Tricky grievance situations

In this chapter, I consider a number of specific situations which might need a particularly nuanced approach. I am not going to explore them in detail; I will just highlight some specific things to consider. This chapter addresses:

- grievances about harassment
- grievances about whistleblowing
- grievances about equal pay
- collective grievances
- grievances about a line manager
- grievances lodged during disciplinary/ performance processes

- employees who go off sick during a grievance process

- malicious or repeat grievances

Grievances about harassment

Harassment is defined in the Equality Act 2010 as "unwanted conduct which has the purpose or effect of violating a person's dignity, or of creating an intimidating, hostile, degrading, humiliating or offensive environment."

To fall within that definition, the harassment must be on the basis of:

- age

- disability

- gender reassignment

- race

- religion or belief

- sex

- sexual orientation

Harassment can be just one single event, or it can be a series of events. It does not have to be directed at an individual for it to be harassment (for example, where an employee is working in an open-plan area and listening to 'banter' that is not directed at that employee but nevertheless creates an intimidating or hostile environment.

It does not matter that the individual did not mean for anyone to take offence at what has been said or done. The question is whether the conduct has had the purpose or effect of harassing the individual. And it follows that there is a certain subjectivity about harassment; what one person sees as a bit of fun might be deeply offensive to someone else.

When managing a grievance that relates to an allegation of harassment, there does need to be some flexibility with regard to whom an employee can first approach if they have a grievance (as the alleged harasser could be their line manager, making it inappropriate to raise the grievance with them). If the alleged harassment is of a sexual nature, they might feel more comfortable raising the grievance with someone of the same sex.

The allegations will have to be investigated, and this could involve talking to a number of witnesses, which might take some time. This could be difficult for the employee if they work closely with the alleged harasser. The action to take will depend on the nature of the allegations. If they are serious, such that it would mean the alleged harasser has done something amounting to gross misconduct, then it might be appropriate to move one of the two people elsewhere temporarily, offer the complainant the chance to work from home or a period of paid leave while the complaint is being investigated, or even suspend the alleged harasser.

Grievances about whistleblowing

'Whistleblowing' is the shorthand word for making a protected disclosure under the Public Interest Disclosure Act 1998. This applies if someone raises an issue that they reasonably believe is in the public interest, and if the employee raising the issue reasonably believes it tends to show a criminal offence, a breach of a legal obligation, or a risk to health and safety.

Grievances that affect just the individual (such as a claim of bullying) are unlikely to be covered under the whistleblowing legislation, because the employee is unlikely to hold a reasonable belief that disclosure of the bullying is in the public interest. However, if a number of employees claim that they are being bullied and the organisation is in the public eye, such a grievance could potentially amount to whistleblowing.

If an individual wants to make a protected disclosure, it should be made in the first instance to the employer or to an appropriate regulatory body (e.g. a health and safety concern would be raised with the Health and Safety Executive). Making a claim to the newspapers (for example) would not, except in very, very limited circumstances, be a protected disclosure.

If an employee does make a protected disclosure, they must not suffer any detriment, or be dismissed, for making the disclosure. This applies even if the disclosure is investigated and it is subsequently found that the disclosure is not well founded.

Equal pay

Equal pay claims arise when a man and woman do:

- like work (basically, they do the same job)
- work of equal value (they do different work, but the 'value' of the job to the organisation is the same)
- work rated as equivalent (the organisation has undertaken an analytical job evaluation scheme – meaning that the different parts of the job are given numerical values – and the ratings are the same).

If the man and the woman do like work, work of equal value or work rated as equivalent and are not receiving the same reward, they can make an equal pay claim. Note that there should be parity in each element of reward. It cannot be argued that the man has a higher salary, but the woman has a greater holiday entitlement, therefore it all balances out.

If an employee raises a grievance that amounts to an equal pay claim, it needs careful analysis. The employer needs to decide if the work is like work, work of equal value or work rated as equivalent. Then, if it is, the employer needs to look at the rate of reward and determine if it is the same or different. If it is different, the employer needs to explore whether it is justifiable.

Collective grievances

Paragraph 47 of the Code of Practice states:

47. The provisions of this Code do not apply to grievances raised on behalf of two or more employees by a representative of a recognised trade union or other appropriate workplace representative. These grievances should be handled in accordance with the organisation's collective grievance process.

A collective grievance is when more than one employee raises the same grievance. For example, it could be a group of employees raising a grievance relating to a change in shift pattern, or in relation to a manager who is perceived to be a bully.

If a trade union representative, or elected employee representative, raises the grievance with management, it should be managed through the processes that have been agreed for discussions between the representatives and management.

If the grievance is raised by one or two employees on behalf of a group of employees, and they are not formally elected representatives, the matter can still be investigated by liaising with them as informal representatives. However, it is also important to keep control of the communication, and management should communicate with all employees affected, explaining the actions being taken.

Grievances about a line manager

Sometimes, employees just do not get on with their line manager. It could be that there is a specific problem, or it could be that they just clash repeatedly. These can be amongst the most complex grievances to investigate, partly because you don't want to set a precedent of an employee 'choosing' their manager, and partly because it's very difficult – particularly if both sides have different recollections of what has occurred – to establish the truth and decide where, if anywhere, the fault lies.

In a large organisation this problem might be resolved by moving either the employee or the line manager to another role. In a small organisation this is less likely to be possible. Even if it seems that the situation is going to be impossible to resolve, it is essential to investigate the situation and give some options to the employee.

Early intervention by an accredited mediator could also be considered in these instances. Such action could prevent the situation from escalating and potentially being litigated. This could also be an outcome of the grievance, although mediation is often the best approach before going through the formal process.

USDAW v Burns (2014) EAT/0557/12

The employee had raised grievances that his line manager was bullying him and setting unreasonable targets. In particular, he identified four specific incidents which he said involved unreasonable behaviour. Despite raising a number of grievances, no action had been taken. He went off sick, was absent for over a year and eventually was dismissed.

The dismissal was unfair because the employer had not done enough to investigate the grievances, and had not considered whether there were any alternative roles the employee could have been moved to.

Grievances lodged during disciplinary/performance management processes

Paragraph 46 of the Code of Practice states:

Where an employee raises a grievance during a disciplinary process, the disciplinary process may be temporarily suspended in order to deal with the grievance. Where the grievance and disciplinary cases are related, it may be appropriate to deal with both issues concurrently.

It is not uncommon to begin addressing an issue using the performance management or the disciplinary process and then have the employee raise a grievance. Sometimes, this is a stalling or deflection tactic, with the employee hoping that raising the grievance will result in the disciplinary situation being overlooked. However, it could also be a genuine situation. For example, the employee may not have raised a grievance so far because they have been scared to do so. The issue being addressed may have given the employee the opportunity to raise a concern.

Broadly, if the grievance covers the same ground as the disciplinary (or performance) issue, you would not normally put the disciplinary on hold, but would have the same manager deal with both grievance and disciplinary as part of the same process. If the grievance covers different issues, deal with them concurrently. If the grievance is an attack on the integrity or impartiality of the manager conducting the disciplinary hearing, you have a choice; either put the disciplinary process on hold while investigating the grievance (never a good idea, as it can cause many months of delay), or just switch out to a different person to handle the disciplinary matter. Offer the employee a choice of two or three other people, and if they object to all of them, no tribunal will criticise you for proceeding despite the employee's objections.

I deal with this issue in a lot more detail in my video 'How to Handle Disciplinary, Dismissal and Performance Management Situations', starting at 1:19:15. You can watch the video (and subscribe to my YouTube channel) at bit.ly/dismissalvideo.

Jinadu v Docklands Buses Ltd (2016) UKEAT/0166/16

The employee was a bus driver, and a member of the public had complained about her standard of driving. The employer investigated and found that there were some serious failings, such as pulling out when cars were passing, one-handed driving, clipping kerbs and driving through a red light.

The employee was instructed to attend a driving assessment at the employer's in-house training centre, but refused on several occasions. She was then invited to attend a disciplinary hearing and was told that she could be dismissed. At the hearing, she raised a grievance that the inspector who had reported her was bullying her, and she also raised issues relating to discrimination and pay.

Despite the allegations, the disciplinary proceedings continued and she was dismissed. She claimed it was an unfair dismissal because the disciplinary proceedings continued whilst her grievances were unresolved. The Employment Appeal Tribunal did not accept this. It ruled that it was reasonable to have continued with the disciplinary process whilst the grievance was also considered.

Samuel Smith Old Brewery (Tadcaster) v Marshall and Marshall (2010) UKEAT/0488/09

The employer told its pub managers to reduce staff hours. Two managers refused to do this, and were disciplined. They raised a grievance about the issue, but the disciplinary proceedings continued. They were dismissed for refusing to obey a reasonable management instruction.

The Employment Appeal Tribunal found that this was a fair dismissal. There was no rule that disciplinary proceedings have to be stopped if a grievance is raised.

Going off sick during the process

Once an employee has raised a grievance, there is the possibility that they may go off sick. Very occasionally, this action (along with the grievance) could be part of a deliberate attempt to cause difficulties, particularly if done within the context of a disciplinary or performance management process. Far more often, it will be that the stress of the situation has made the employee unwell.

If this happens the first question is whether the grievance, or circumstances underlying the grievance, are causing the illness. If they are, then it is probably unhelpful to say that you will wait until the employee returns to work to address the grievance. The grievance needs to be addressed to help the employee to recover. Firstly, ask the employee for permission to seek a medical opinion from their doctor (the permission must be in writing), or refer the employee to your own occupational health service. Specifically, ask for a medical opinion on whether the employee is well enough to meet and discuss the grievance.

If the employee is well enough, hold the grievance meeting in much the same way as you would anyway – but give the employee the option of meeting away from the work location and discuss any other process adjustments that might assist the employee to participate. Depending on the situation, it might, for example, be appropriate to exclude witnesses from the process because questioning witnesses can be stressful in itself.

If the employee is not well enough to meet, write to the employee and ask them to make contact as soon as they feel well enough, but also keep in regular contact. If you have enough information about the grievance, then continue with the investigations whilst the employee is absent. If the employee shows no sign of coming back to work in the near future, and your investigations are complete, you could write to the employee with an explanation of your findings and the offer of a meeting to discuss them as soon as the employee is better.

If the employee is disabled, as defined in the Equality Act 2010, you would be required to make reasonable adjustments to the grievance process to help the employee to engage fully.

Malicious or repeat grievances

After investigating a grievance, you might conclude that the complaints are not only unfounded, but that there were no reasonable grounds to raise them in the first place. This may have resulted in a waste of management time and a potentially upsetting time for anyone who has been accused of any wrongdoing as part of the grievance. It should be emphasised that this is rare. As mentioned in Chapter 1, there is usually an element of truth in all grievances. Just because somebody has got the wrong end of the stick – even massively so – does not mean they did not believe what they were saying.

Before taking any action, consider whether the employee could have reasonably thought that the grievance was well founded. It could be that the employee totally misunderstood a situation rather than acted maliciously.

Also consider whether the grievance could be considered a protected disclosure (see earlier in this chapter, where I addressed 'whistleblowing'). If the employee reasonably believed that they were raising a valid issue, even if they were motivated by bad faith, and if it could be a protected disclosure, the employee must not suffer a detriment (which includes any disciplinary action) as a result of raising the issue.

However, if you conclude that it is not a protected disclosure and that there were no real grounds for raising the issue, you could consider taking disciplinary action against the employee.

There should not be a rush to take disciplinary action. Having a quiet word might be action enough. You do not want to communicate to the rest of the workforce that they might be disciplined if they bring a grievance. Keep disciplinary action for the situations in which there really is malicious action.

There are some employees who raise a lot of grievances. They might believe that all are genuine grievances, but if they are not well founded, you need to take some action to stop the continuing raising of grievances. You could tell an employee that they are not allowed to raise any more grievances, and that if they do, you will not consider the grievances they raise. The danger of taking this approach is that something genuine might arise, and you refuse to deal with it. Alternatively, you could try to reason with the employee and agree criteria for what really constitutes a grievance. You could then state that a grievance will only be investigated if it matches the agreed criteria.

Bashir and Bashir v Sheffield Teaching Hospital NHS Foundation Trust (2010) UKEAT/0448/09

A husband and wife who worked for the same organisation raised a number of grievances. They then were uncooperative with the process for resolving the grievances, did not turn up for meetings, argued with the process for hearing the grievances and were generally obstructive. Eventually, they were dismissed. These were found to be fair dismissals. Their behaviour had resulted in a complete breakdown of trust between the employer and the two employees.

CHAPTER 11
Getting it wrong

In the various situations I have looked at in this book, I have considered different outcomes, including claims for constructive dismissal and discrimination. What are the possible consequences if the employer gets these situations wrong?

Constructive dismissal

Constructive dismissal occurs when the employer breaches the contract of employment and the employee resigns in response to that breach, doing so in a timely manner. In a grievance situation it is likely to be argued that the employer has breached the implied contractual term of mutual trust and confidence by not addressing a grievance fairly or promptly.

To bring a claim of constructive dismissal, the employee needs at least two years' continuous service with the employer (unless the reason is one that is automatically unfair, such as the breach relates to being pregnant/on maternity leave, raising a health and safety concern, whistleblowing, or exercising a statutory right).

The remedy is:

- a 'basic' award (which is calculated in exactly the same way as a statutory redundancy payment), plus

- a 'compensatory' award (which looks at the financial loss that the employee has suffered). This is a maximum of the lower of the employee's annual salary, or (as at December 2020, the date of writing) £88,519. This sum increases in line with inflation every April. This cap does not apply if the employee is (constructively) dismissed for whistleblowing.

Discrimination

Discrimination includes:

- direct discrimination (including perceptive and associative)

- indirect discrimination

- harassment

- victimisation (treating someone badly because they've raised issues of discrimination)

- discrimination arising from disability

Woodhouse v West North West Homes Leeds (2013) IRLR 773

The employee had made a number of claims of race discrimination and was eventually dismissed because of a fundamental breakdown in the employment relationship. He argued that this was victimisation because he was being dismissed due to the number of discrimination claims that he had brought.

He was successful in his claim.

An employee does not need any qualifying service to bring a claim of discrimination.

The compensation which can be awarded is unlimited, and it will broadly reflect the employee's loss of earnings resulting from the discrimination. However, unlike unfair dismissal awards, there is also an amount awarded for injury to feelings. The injury to feelings awards, at the time of writing (December 2020) are:-

- one-off acts of discrimination: £900 to £9,000

- most other cases, typically including dismissals: £9,000 to £27,000

- the most serious cases, often involving conduct over many years: £27,000 to £45,000

Appendix 1
Model Grievance Policy

This is from www.policies2020.com, a website from which you can purchase and download a pack of twenty model employment policies written by the author of this book, Daniel Barnett.

1. Overview

1.1 This policy helps us deal with complaints, concerns, and problems to do with employment fairly and consistently. Please note that this policy only applies to matters relating to your employment. If you have a separate relationship, such as being a customer or service user, you must use a separate process for concerns.

1.2 This policy applies to all employees, but does not form part of your employment contract, and we may update it at any time.

1.3 You should only use this procedure to raise a grievance connected with your employment. Complaints made against you will normally be dealt with under our Disciplinary Policy or Performance Improvement Policy, as appropriate.

1.4 You should also look at our Harassment and Bullying Policy and our Whistleblowing Policy, both of which might be relevant.

1.5 Most grievances are raised individually, but if a group of employees bring substantially the same grievance, we will address it as a group grievance and follow the process described below.

2. Taking informal action

2.1 You should approach your manager before doing anything else, as we find most grievances can be resolved informally. If your grievance is about your manager — or there is some other reason you don't want to raise it with them — you must instead notify their line manager or somebody else holding the same level of responsibility as your manager.

2.2 If this informal approach does not resolve your problem, you should use the formal procedure.

3. Taking formal action: First stage

3.1   You will need to set out the details of your complaint in writing. Include dates, names of individuals involved, and any other relevant facts, and tell us clearly that you want to lodge a formal grievance. It will be helpful if you set out any steps you have taken to resolve the issue informally.

3.2   You must also explain clearly what you want to see the Company do. You could for example say: 'I want you to issue a warning to (the name of the individual you are complaining about)', or: 'I want you to change your policy on overtime working.'

3.3   Send or hand your written grievance to [your line manager] [or] [the HR department]. If your line manager is part of your grievance, you should send your grievance to [their line manager, or to] [NAME].

3.4   We will write to you to let you know that we've received your grievance.

3.5   You must co-operate with us to ensure our investigation is fair and thorough. How we investigate will depend on the nature of your grievance. We will look at relevant documents and may interview you and/or take a statement from you and from other people able to provide information.

4. Taking formal action: Second stage

4.1 We will invite you to a meeting, usually within [five working days] [or] [x days/weeks] of you lodging your grievance. The meeting is your opportunity to explain your problem and how you think we should resolve it, and we ask that you make every effort to attend.

4.2 You can bring a companion with you to the meeting — this will typically be a work colleague or a trade union representative (full details in paragraph 6 below). You must let us know as soon as possible if either you or your companion is unable to attend the meeting and we will try to reschedule.

4.3

[either]

[Please do not record the meeting without our consent, as this suggests that you do not trust the Company's process or the managers who are conducting it. [We may decide to deal with covert recording as a disciplinary matter.]

If you have misgivings about either the process or the managers leading it, you should tell us openly so that we can address your concerns. For our part, we in turn will not record the meeting without your knowledge.]

[or]

[We may record the meeting, but we will not do so without telling you. You are welcome to record the meeting if you wish, but please tell us as we think it is discourteous to the managers involved for you to make a covert recording. You will also get a better quality recording if you do it openly rather than covertly.]

4.4 After the meeting, we will take any steps to investigate further that we consider appropriate. Sometimes this will involve looking at documents or interviewing other people. We will not normally allow you to take part in this part of the investigation (for example, you will not normally be allowed to question other people directly). Sometimes, we may ask you for more information or for another meeting. And sometimes, we may think there is no need for any further investigation.

4.5 Within a week of the final meeting (this may be the first or the second meeting, depending on the circumstances) we will write to you with our decision and let you know if we plan to take any action to address your grievance. We will also tell you who to write to if you want to appeal our decision (paragraph 5 below). In complicated grievances, or if the manager hearing your grievance is very busy, it may take longer than a week to make our decision and prepare an outcome letter. If that happens, we will keep you informed about the likely timescales.

4.6 Sometimes, we may decide it is inappropriate to discuss some, or even all, of the steps we are taking as the result of your grievance with you (usually because the other person involved might have an entitlement to confidentiality, which has to be balanced against your right to know what has happened). We recognise that will leave you feeling dissatisfied, and we would only do this if there was a good reason not to keep you informed.

5. Taking formal action: Third stage

5.1 If you are not happy with our decision, you can appeal in writing within one week of us giving you the decision. Your appeal letter [or email] must explain clearly why you are appealing. You should also give us any new evidence you may have acquired since the initial investigation was completed.

5.2 We will invite you to a meeting, usually within two weeks of you lodging your appeal. Wherever possible, the appeal meeting will not be led by the manager who held the original grievance meeting. You may be accompanied by a trade union representative or work colleague, in line with the process outlined in paragraph 6 below.

5.3 Our final decision will be sent to you in writing. We try to do this within two weeks of the appeal hearing. You do not have any further right to appeal against our decision.

6. Your right to be accompanied

6.1 You are entitled to be accompanied by a colleague or trade union representative at any meeting called under this policy.

6.2 If you want to exercise this right, you should tell us as soon as possible who you want to accompany you. It is your responsibility to arrange for them to attend. If you choose a work colleague, we will not prevent them from attending, but we may rearrange the meeting if their absence from work would cause operational problems.

6.3 Your colleague or trade union representative can, if you'd like them to, explain the key points of your grievance at the meeting and can respond on your behalf. You can also confer with them during the meetings. However, they must not answer questions put directly to you or try to prevent us asking questions or outlining our views.

Appendix 2

Sources of further help

In complex grievances, if the employer lacks the internal resources to conduct a detailed investigation, the employer can engage an outsourced independent consultant to advise on the grievance process, or conduct the full investigation and produce a report.

I am sometimes able to help supervise or run the grievance process in very complex cases, particularly where there may be high (six or seven figure) litigation as a potential outcome. You can find out more via my clerks at www.outertemple.com.

More commonly, employers will use an independent HR consultant. Fees vary depending on location and experience, but rates are typically £500 - £750 per day. You can find my list of independent HR consultants, all of whom are experienced in conducting investigations, at bit.ly/grievanceinvestigations.

Also by
Daniel Barnett

JOIN DANIEL EVERY SATURDAY EVENING
AT 9PM WHEN HE PRESENTS THE

LBC LEGAL HOUR

— OR CATCH UP VIA THE GLOBAL PLAYER,
AT bit.ly/lbclegalhour

SATURDAYS, 9PM

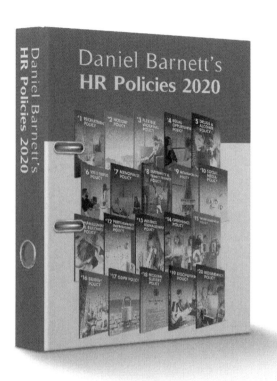

I have updated my 20 Employment Law Policies for small businesses.

If you are an HR professional, they are perfect for incorporating into a staff handbook. If you are a solicitor, they come with a licence for you to resell them or give them away for free to clients.

WWW.POLICIES2020.COM

HR INNER CIRCLE

"The HR Inner Circle has improved my life amazingly,

mainly because it means I have to spend less time researching and more time and more time actually doing the work I'm paid for."

Sue Whittle, Employment & Safety Advice LTD

Join to gain access to the monthly HR Inner Circular magazine

jam-packed with amazing information for ambitious HR professionals

WWW.HRINNERCIRCLE.CO.UK

What do you get?

1 Monthly live online 'Ask Me Anything' sessions: each month, we host an online video webinar, when you can share your HR problems and ask Daniel anything about employment law. You'll also receive a recording and a transcript each month, so you have a permanent record of the session even if you cannot be there.

HR — DANIEL BARNETT'S —
INNER CIRCLE

Please ask your questions now:
1. click 'Raise Hand'; or,
2. type it into the Questions box

> "Daniel Barnett is an inspirational, walking and talking 'how to understand mind-boggling employment law handbook!"

Ellie King, HR Manager, RWE Technology

2 A specially recorded audio seminar every month, with HR shortcuts and workarounds you can't get anywhere else.

3 The monthly Inner Circular magazine, jam-packed with valuable information for ambitious HR professionals.

4 Access to Daniel's exclusive, private, invitation-only online Inner Circle group, where you get to discuss HR problems with other smart, ambitious professionals and download precedents and policies they have shared.

"It's the support and help that you get, the reassurance that you're talking to people who know what they're talking about rather than people just randomly giving information."

Nicky Jolley, HR2DAY LTD

5 Access to the exclusive HR Inner Circle website which includes a back-catalogue of all the HRIC resources since the launch in 2015.

WWW.HRINNERCIRCLE.CO.UK

"This is one of the best investments in yourself and your career you will ever decide to take."

100%
Risk-Free
Guarantee

Only **£86 + VAT**
per month

No long-term contracts.
No notice periods.
No fuss.

Join today!

WWW.HRINNERCIRCLE.CO.UK

If you are looking for a forum to discuss confidential issues that need prompt employment law advice, then the HR Inner Circle is definitely for you. In addition it offers other tools to help and support. The Facebook group is full of information and solutions to scenarios — invaluable for HR professionals.

- **Sheena Doyle**, Managing Director, The Really Useful HR Company Ltd

It's a forum where you're not afraid to ask stupid questions, even though I'm not usually afraid of doing that. The sheer variety of experience and skillsets ensures there is always an informed discussion. JOIN NOW!!

- **Jon Dews**, HR & Business Partner, Majestic 12 Ltd

If you are looking for a steady stream of thorough, pragmatic, and easily-digestible employment law advice, the HR Inner Circle is a great place to be.

- **Susi O'Brien**, Senior Manager HR, The Action Group

The regular updates are invaluable to not only me, but also my team. We find that they are presented in an easy to digest format and aren't too 'legalistic'.

- **Donna Negus**, Sekoya Specialist Employment Services

There aren't many other employment law advice services where you get direct access to an employment law barrister at a realistic price. Join the HR Inner Circle now – you won't regret it.

- **Kirsten Cluer**, Owner of Cluer HR, HR Consultancy

I like being able to use the HR Inner Circle Facebook group to ask other members for a second opinion, or for ideas when I get stuck with solving a tricky situation. There's usually someone who has come across the situation before.

- **Helen Astill**, Managing Director, Cherington HR Ltd

When I transitioned from big employers to an SME, I didn't realise how much I would miss having peers to kick ideas around. If you haven't got an internal network, you've got to build an external one. I got so much out of the discussion at an Inner Circle meetup recently and I look forward to getting the Inner Circular.

- **Elizabeth Divver**, Group HR Director, The Big Issue Group

Sign now! The monthly Q & A sessions are invaluable, the magazine is packed full of helpful info, you get lots of goodies and the Facebook page is really informative and a useful sounding board.

- **Caroline Hitchen**, Consultant, Caroline Neal Employment Law

Being a member of HR Inner Circle is one of the best sources of HR information and advice, and receiving the monthly audio seminars and magazines is extremely helpful and interesting. I can't recommend becoming a member highly enough. There is a private Facebook group which is great for asking other members advice and sharing knowledge and experiences. I have also recently attended one of the meetups that is organised by Daniel Barnett, and it was good to meet other members (and of course Daniel) in a more social setting. It was also a good opportunity to ask any questions you wanted and being able to get advice or support as to how they would deal with whatever you ask.

- **Tracey Seymour**, HR Manager (Head of Dept), Kumon Europe & Africa Ltd

The help and advice from other HR professionals on Facebook is really valuable, and quick. All the team enjoy the audio seminars and magazines for updates on current issues.

- **Catherine Larke**, Director | myHRdept.co.uk

For me it's a no brainer. We have a lot of really good contributors in the HR Inner Circle and it's more than a discussion forum and invaluable source of information. When combined with the magazine, the audio seminars and events, it is a complete service especially with Daniel's legal expertise always on hand.

- **Elizabeth Ince**, Self employed HR Consultant

Just join! It is invaluable with the resources you have at hand by joining the HR Inner Circle. Especially the Facebook Group where you can get advice or a different point of view that you may not have previously considered, outside of normal working hours which is very useful. Live Q&A's too.

- **Diana Wilks**, HR Manager, Go South Coast Ltd

HR can be complex because each and every issue will have its own set of individual circumstances. Being in the HR Inner Circle enables you to bounce ideas around and make sure you are considering every angle and aspect, knowing your HR Inner Circle partners will have had a similar experience to share.

- **Pam Rogerson**, HR Director, ELAS Group

Printed in Great Britain
by Amazon